ABOUT THE BOOK

Ostriches are the largest birds in the world. They are not flying birds, but they can run fast and defend themselves with their strong legs. They grow to be about 8 feet tall and·weigh up to 300 pounds.

Wallace Litwin focuses on a family of ostriches in Africa: the courting of several females by a male bird to lay eggs in an enormous nest; the banishment of the other females by the strongest female; the long incubation period; the birth of the babies; and their first weeks, learning to survive.

Detailed photographs record each event. Among the most dramatic is a step-by-step sequence of a baby ostrich breaking out of the tough skin and shell of a large egg and giving his ''call of triumph.''

A fascinating account of one of the world's unusual creatures.

OSTRICH

written and photographed by

WALLACE LITWIN

COWARD, McCANN & GEOGHEGAN, INC.   NEW YORK

SBN: GB-698-30505-1
SBN: TR-698-20253-8
Library of Congress Catalog Card Number: 72-94276
Designed by Bobye List
8 up
PRINTED IN THE UNITED STATES OF AMERICA
Second Impression

To Struthio Camelus,
and all the other delightful birds.

Ostriches are the largest birds in the world. They live on the sandy plains of Africa and in the deserts of Arabia. This bird lives in Central Africa.

Male ostriches are eight feet tall and weigh about three hundred pounds. They are much bigger than any man. The females are almost as tall as the males and they weigh about fifty pounds less. The males have black feathers edged with white. The females are pure brown, like this one.

Most of the time, these large birds move in groups of twenty or thirty. They live side by side with antelopes, zebras, and wild cattle. These animals share the same water holes peacefully.

During the mating season, ostriches break up into smaller groups of birds, usually one male and three females.

When a male sees a female he wants in his group, he sings her his courtship song. It sounds like "Boo Boo <u>Boooh</u> Hoo." He sings it over and over again in a low, throaty voice. If the female isn't interested in him, she doesn't pay any attention to him.

If she likes him, she sings back, and they begin to dance.

Only during the mating dance does the male ostrich fan out his beautiful white tail feathers and stand them straight up. This is his signal to other males that he and a female are about to mate and they must stay away from her.

Mating takes place toward the end of the dry season in the fall, before the rains begin. If the eggs got wet and cold, no baby ostriches would hatch.

A male usually mates with three females. The hens help him scoop out an eight- or nine-foot-wide nest in the sand. Each hen will lay about eight eggs in this nest. The eggs weigh from a pound and a half to three pounds, depending on how old the hen is and how healthy she is. From these twenty-four eggs about fifteen to twenty chicks will hatch.

While the eggs are being laid, the male guards the nest. Most of these two weeks he sits nearby, preening his feathers and dust-bathing. During the hot midday, he sits on the eggs to shade them from the sun. If the eggs get hotter than 99 degrees, they will not hatch.

When the eggs have been laid, the "major hen," who is the oldest and strongest, drives the other two hens from the nest. These younger birds, called minor hens, are no longer allowed to come near the eggs.

The major hen and the male ostrich will incubate and hatch the eggs. They will be the birds' only parents.

The male bird plays no part in choosing the mother hen. But he accepts her as his nest mate for the forty-five days of incubation that are about to start.

During this period, the parents must protect the eggs from other animals who would eat them: snakes that can swallow them whole, buzzards and hawks that can break them with their talons, and small animals that can suck them dry.

When another animal comes too close, the father hisses and scowls to scare his enemy away.

The mother bird looks good-natured and content. But if anything approaches the nest, she can be as fierce as the male.

The mother hen sits on the eggs during most of the day. The male bird stands guard ready to attack any intruders. If there is danger near the nest, the mother bird hisses out a warning. At night, the male sits on the eggs.

During this incubation period, the eggs must be kept at body temperature. The eggs can be left exposed to the warm sun during the cool parts of the day. But at midday when the sun is at its hottest, they must be protected.

The eggs have to be turned occasionally. When the birds are standing, they turn the eggs with their beaks. But it is usually done seated with a squirming motion of the body.

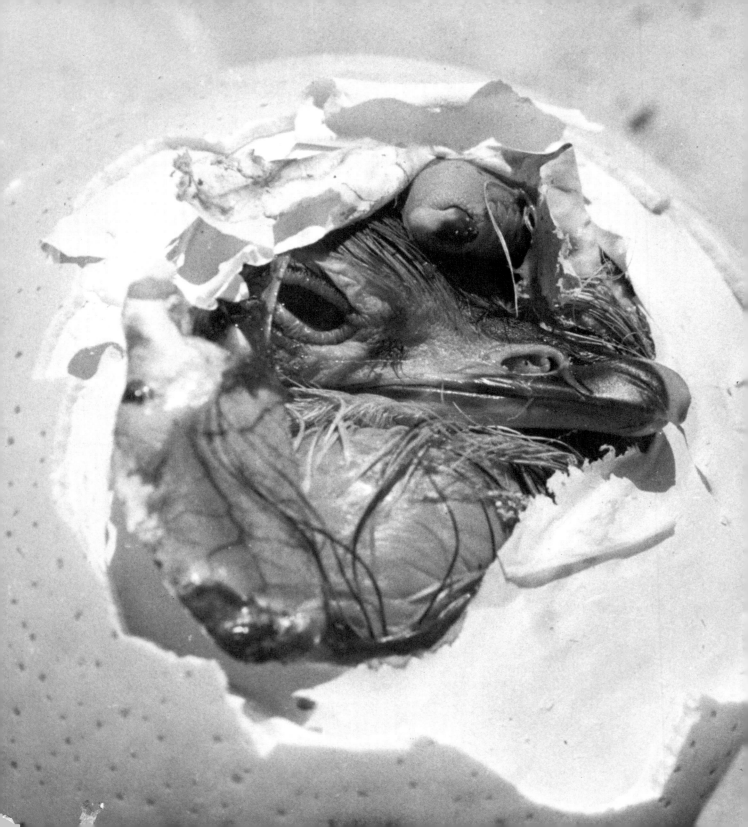

For more than six weeks, the baby ostrich chicks have been growing inside the eggs. Now their tiny bodies fill every bit of space inside the shells. The only place to go is out.

When the chicks make musical piping sounds inside the eggs, the parents know that the hatching is about to begin. The first cracking of the eggs makes such a loud noise that the bird sometimes jumps off the nest in fright.

Slowly the baby chick uses its beak and claws to escape. The parents cannot help because their large, clumsy beaks might crush the egg and hurt the baby. The baby ostrich must do all the work himself.

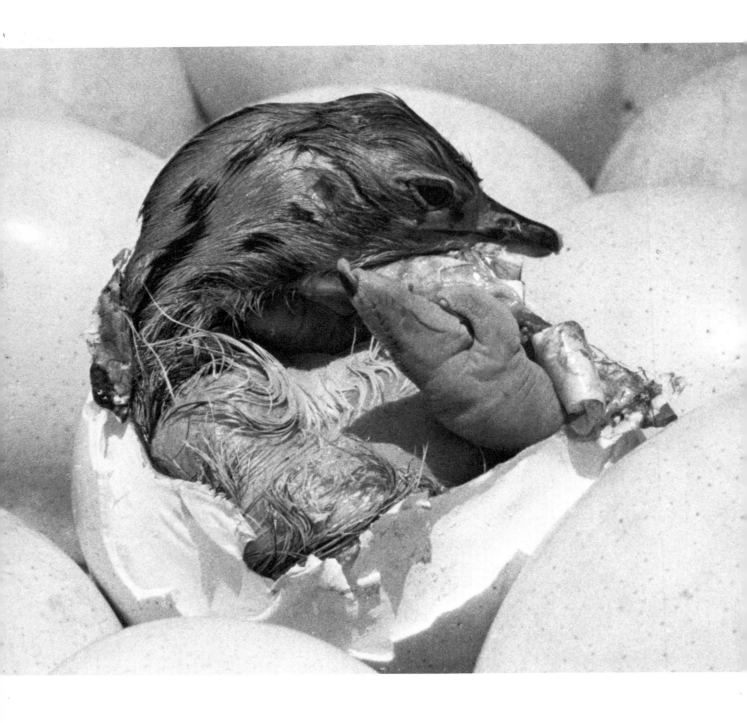

Inside the egg, the baby ostrich has been enclosed in a layer of skin which held nourishing liquid. This liquid and the yolk have been his only food. The little bird uses all the strength of his big foot to rip the skin and roll it back.

Halfway out of the shell, the wet baby chick is worn-out. He takes a rest and soaks up some warm sun.

When the baby ostrich has his head out of the shell completely and his neck stretched out for the first time, he makes a shrill peep. This is known as the "call of triumph."

An hour after breaking out of the shell, the baby's body is still the shape of the egg. It takes a couple of days for him to start being shaped like an ostrich.

The mother hen guards the eggs and protects the chick from enemies while he dries in the sun.

After a few hours, he is still not completely dry. But he is already trying to stand on his big, clumsy feet.

At one day old, he is beginning to look more like an ostrich.

The baby chicks snuggle under the male's warm feathers. The father makes his most terrifying face. Only a foolish fox or snake would try to rob this nest.

Now the baby ostrich is five days old.

Relaxed and warmed by the sun, he sits chirping happily with his twins. After being alone for many weeks inside an egg, he now finds himself surrounded by fifteen brothers and sisters.

As he grows, he begins to look more like his parents. His small wings look like little arms. Ostriches cannot fly and their wings never grow large like most birds'. Ostriches use their wings to keep their balance while running.

An ostrich's legs are very strong right from the beginning. They are his only defense against enemies. He can't fly. He has no teeth to bite with, and his soft beak is useless for pecking. But his legs are tremendous. He can run very fast, and he can use them to kick with. If necessary, he can kill an enemy by kicking.

At two weeks, the little birds are the same color as the sand and brush of the African desert. Flying hawks and other birds who would like to swoop down and make a meal of them cannot see them easily.

To a hungry bird flying overhead he looks like a small bush.

The parents make their chicks walk and run constantly for the first two or three months so that when they grow up their huge legs will be straight and strong. A herd of zebras grazes in the background.

The chicks are learning how to find food to nourish their fast-growing bodies. Ostriches eat grass and other plants, insects, small reptiles like frogs, lizards, and snakes, and other small animals like mice. Since they have no teeth, they swallow pebbles, which stay in their stomachs and help grind up the food.

The family takes shelter from the hot noon sun in the shade of a palm tree.

The best part of the day is a stop at the water hole for a drink.
Ostriches never swim or bathe. They take dust baths to keep clean.

The little chick will live with his mother and father and his brothers and sisters for about a year. At the start of the breeding season, he will be big enough to join the main ostrich flock, where he will stay for another year or two.

When he is old enough to compete with other young males, he will look for three attractive hens. If they respond when he sings, they will dance and mate.

Then he will become the father of a family of baby chicks and the cycle will begin again.

ABOUT THE AUTHOR

World-traveling photographer Wallace Litwin, while between assignments, was told that a family of African ostriches was preparing to nest nearby. It was a chance to spend the next forty-five days "sitting" with them and photographing the event.

"Nothing could have been more important to me. I got an old Jeep and spent the daylight hours of the following month and a half standing on the motor hood with my cameras, putting it all on film.

"Occasionally the male bird got annoyed and tried to run me off; but his beak was too soft for pecking, and he couldn't kick higher than the fenders, so I was safe enough. But the fenders got kicked to ribbons.

"Once he managed to jump onto the hood, and I had to hop off on the far side and hide underneath until he went away, soon, luckily, since the ants were trying to bite me to death."

Travel and photography are work and play for Mr. Litwin, whose work has appeared in many magazines, here and abroad. They include *Town and Country, Life, New York, Vogue, Esquire, Harper's Bazaar,* and others.

Wallace Litwin is a New Yorker, born and bred.